Shaping the Church from the Mind of Christ

Shaping the Church from the Mind of Christ

A Study of Paul's Letter to the Philippians

Edward L. Tullis

THE UPPER ROOM
Nashville, Tennessee

Shaping the Church from the Mind of Christ

Copyright © 1984 by The Upper Room.
All rights reserved.

The lines from *SPHERE, the Form of a Motion,* by A. R. Ammons are reprinted by permission of W. W. Norton and Co. Inc., copyright © 1974 by A. R. Ammons.

The scripture quotations not otherwise identified and the text of Paul's Letter to the Philippians that appears at the back of the book are from the Revised Standard Version of the Bible, copyrighted 1946, 1952, © 1971, 1973 by the Division of Christian Education of the National Council of the Churches of Christ in the U.S.A., and are used by permission.

The initials KJV are used throughout this book to identify quotations from the King James Version of the Bible.

Quotations from the *Good News Bible, The Bible in Today's English Version* (TEV), copyright by American Bible Society 1966, 1971, © 1976, are used by permission.

Scripture quotations designated Moffatt are from *The Bible: A New Translation* by James Moffatt. Copyright, 1935 by Harper & Row, Publishers, Inc., By permission of the publisher.

Scripture quotations designated Phillips are from *The New Testament in Modern English,* by J. B. Phillips, and are reprinted with permission of the Macmillan Company. Copyright © 1958 by J. B Phillips.

Painting on the cover is by Jerry Dunnam
Book Design: Harriette Bateman
First Printing: April, 1984(8)
Library of Congress Catalog Card Number: 84-50837
ISBN: 0-8358-0494-1
Printed in the United States of America

This book is dedicated to
WILLIAM EDGAR CASSELL
(1904-1980)
superb teacher and preacher of the Word,
who literally "opened" the Bible
for several generations of students
first at Kentucky Wesleyan College
and then at Kansas Wesleyan University.

Contents

Preface *9*

1. The Gospel Comes to Europe *11*
   ACTS 16:6-40

2. Finding Our Identity with Christ *15*
   PHILIPPIANS 1:1-11 AND 2:5

3. Proclaiming the Gospel of Christ. *25*
   PHILIPPIANS 1:12-26

4. What Christ Expects of His Church *31*
   PHILIPPIANS 1:27-2:18

5. What It Means to Know Christ *45*
   PHILIPPIANS 3:1-21

6. Christ and the Future *53*
   PHILIPPIANS 4:1-23

   Conclusion *61*

   References for Additional Study. *63*

   The Letter of Paul to the Phillippians. *65*
   Complete Text (RSV)

Preface

For the past forty-six years of my ministry it has been my privilege to share in Bible studies with the parishes to which I have been related. As a pastor of a local church for thirty-five years, and now as a general superintendent for eleven years, I have tried to give a major emphasis to the teaching of the Word.

Paul's letter to the Philippians has always been a special source of inspiration. The basic materials in this study have been shared with many groups whose response has even heightened my interest. I have especially enjoyed participating in these studies with the Southeastern Jurisdiction Convocation on Aging at Lake Junaluska, North Carolina, in 1982. Later in that same year I spent the better part of a day with this letter with the clergy of our church in Estonia, U.S.S.R., during an episcopal visit in the Northern European Area with Bishop Ole Borgen. How could one better illustrate Paul's admonition to the Philippians, "Stand firm thus in the Lord" (4:1), than by simply telling of the sturdy faith of those servants of Christ who have been faithful across the years? That day of teaching will long be with me!

A joyous weekend with this study was spent with the all-church retreat of the Belmont United Methodist Church of Nashville at Beersheba Springs, Tennessee. Weeks of sharing the material in this letter with Dr. Thomas Langford of Duke

Divinity School were times of rare fellowship and insight.

My gratitude goes to several who read this manuscript and helped me with its final form: Dr. R. Wright Spears of Lake Junaluska, North Carolina, who read and evaluated my efforts; Dr. Maxie Dunnam, Senior Minister of Christ United Methodist Church, Memphis, Tennessee, who made valuable suggestions concerning content; Ms. Charla Honea, Ms. Janice Grana and Ms. Mary Ruth Coffman of the Upper Room Staff, whose counsel was given generously; Ms. Carolyn Simms, who spent hours checking grammatical constructions; and Mrs. Marie Thompson, who efficiently typed and typed again the manuscript.

My deepest gratitude goes to Mary Jane, with whom I have shared forty-six years in a ministry she has deeply enriched with her counsel and companionship.

EDWARD L. TULLIS

1

The Gospel Comes to Europe

Acts 16:6-40

It was a memorable day in the growth of the Christian movement when the apostle Paul and his companions arrived at Philippi. The gospel was being preached in Europe for the first time, as far as we know. A new congregation would begin, which was to have a close relationship with Paul across the years. Evidently several letters were exchanged between Paul and the Philippians during later years. The New Testament Letter to the Philippians, with which we shall deal in this book, records a part of two or more letters from Paul to this congregation.

It is interesting to discover from the account in Acts 16 that Paul had not intended to go to Philippi or even to Europe at this particular time. He and Silas, and probably Luke, set out to extend the ministry of the gospel in Asia. Hindered by all kinds of obstacles (Acts 16:6-8), Paul was visited one night in a dream by a Macedonian who pleaded, "Come over to Macedonia and help us."

Believing that the Spirit was guiding them, the team heeded the vision and changed directions, heading for Europe on the *Via Egnatia,* the great Roman road from Asia to the main points of Europe. Along the way they stopped at Philippi, a city in northern Greece. It was a strategic spot set in a range of hills dividing Europe and Asia.

At Philippi, no Macedonian awaited them with a welcoming

address. In fact, their first opportunity to witness for Christ came on the Sabbath when they met by the riverside with a group of devout women for a prayer service. Here Paul had his first convert in Europe, a woman named Lydia, prominent in business in the area. After she and her family were baptized and received into the church, she evidently made her home available as the first center for the Christian community in Philippi.

What a dramatic moment this was for that first-century church—and for us. The spread of the gospel was underway in Europe! The momentum changed from moving toward Asia and began to move into Greece and Rome. What a significant step this was. As the mission spread through Europe, civilization was being changed. Europe was being influenced by the message of Christ, and Christian descendants found their way to America and put the stamp of the faith on a new nation. What a difference, had Paul and Silas moved on toward Asia. Indeed, this first prayer meeting and first convert in Europe was a red-letter event. But, on with the startling events at Philippi!

Paul soon found himself in a conflict. A young slave girl, used as a soothsayer by some local businessmen, was attracted by the good news of a nobler way of living. God's grace brought peace and serenity to her troubled spirit, but her occult powers were lost. Disturb business practices and you have a confrontation! Paul did. He and Silas were arrested, beaten, and thrown in jail.

Unusual things began to occur. During a midnight session of song and prayer, an earthquake opened prison doors. The jailer, thinking his captives had escaped, prepared to commit suicide, only to be stopped by these strange preachers. Deeply moved by all he had seen and heard, the jailer experienced God's saving grace. He, his wife, and his children became part of the infant congregation.

Soon, Paul departed because of persecution, leaving behind at Philippi this fledgling congregation. They had little nurture in the faith, and the group was widely diverse—a prominent business woman and her family, a rough-hewn political appointee and his kin, a still-mystified slave girl, and a group of women later named in the Philippian letter. Any chance for a growing church? Our present-day surveys assure us that Philippi would not be a likely place for a viable congregation. Some people would maintain that such diverse elements with different cultural backgrounds could not become an active, unified congregation. Moreover, severe persecution made it unlikely that these new converts would hold out. You couldn't expect much to happen in Philippi.

But in spite of all adversity, the new community of faith grew in courage and conviction. From time to time, Paul sent his co-workers to minister to them. Though Paul's visit was abbreviated, he had laid the foundation. A fellowship within the group and with the continuing Christian mission was established. Time and distance could not break the ties, and frequently the small congregation sent gifts to Paul and his companions who labored on the frontiers of the faith.

It is to this remarkable community of faith that Paul writes his letter of gratitude which expands to a call to radiant faith. It is not a dissertation from an ivory tower. He writes from captivity, yet his message is filled with joy. The word *joy* is found sixteen times in the four brief chapters. His living union with his Lord, his commitment to "the mind of Christ," reveals unlimited resources of power. Though waiting for a possible death sentence, he is not in despair. Peace and joy experienced from the grace of God enable him to look to the future with faith and to share his secret of strength with his friends.

This letter may well set the agenda for the Body of Christ today. When we are influenced so much by our secular cultural values and are so misdirected by voices far removed from the motivation of the mind of the Master, we need to set our own minds on the spirit and attitude so clearly revealed in this letter from one who has deeply communed with Christ. In so doing, we may understand more clearly what it could mean for us to have the mind of Christ in the church today.

For Discussion at the Close of Chapter 1

1. How would you evaluate the change in the direction of the Christian mission as it moved toward Europe instead of penetrating further into what we today call the Middle East?

2. What elements do you see in the early account of this Philippian congregation that united them in spite of the obvious diversity in their background and experience?

3. Is it possible for us to experience Christian fellowship in our churches with the kind of diversity that was evident in this early church?

4. What factors in Paul's life do you suppose enabled him to experience prison life and yet write to the Philippians with such a sense of confidence and joy?

2

Finding Our Identity with Christ

Philippians 1:1-11; 2:5

LET THIS MIND BE IN YOU, WHICH WAS ALSO IN CHRIST JESUS.
—2:5, KJV

A few years ago a book-length poem by Archie Ammons contained this interesting insight:

> . . . Some people when they get up in the morning see
> the kitchen sink, but I look out and see the windy rivers
> of the Lord in the treetops: you have your identity when
> you find out not what you can keep your mind on but what
> you can't keep your mind off.[1]

I think Paul would have agreed with that judgment. For years now he has been unable to keep his mind off the mind of Christ. The amazing attitude and spirit of Christ has more and more captivated Paul's thinking and direction.

It seems to me that the entire letter to the Philippians is an exposition of what it means to possess and be possessed of that mind of Christ. This mind transforms Paul personally. It dominates the spirit and direction of Paul's associates as they move out in mission.

[1]Archie Ammons, *Sphere* (New York: W. W. Norton, 1974), pp. 57-58.

It is this approach to ministry that causes folks to identify these early Christian leaders as those "who have turned the world upside down" (Acts 17:6). Their manner, their methods, their sense of values were so different from the cultural patterns of that first-century world that they were seen by their contemporaries as mad persons or dangerous revolutionaries. Just as the mind and presence of Christ disturbed folks in his day (see Luke 8:37), so these followers of Christ were seen as upsetters.

Paul calls upon his beloved community at Philippi to set their mind, their spirit, their agenda, and their mission from the mind of Christ. The entire letter takes this direction. It calls for the church to get the "Christ mind-set," to manifest that spirit in all of the life of the church, and to proclaim this life-changing message to a world set entirely in a different direction.

In these studies, we will look at what Paul conceives to be the makeup of this mind and spirit. We will try not only to see what the Christ-mind meant in the first century, but what it might mean to the body of Christian believers today. If somehow we become so enchanted with, and captivated by, this marvelous mind of Christ, which was sensed so clearly by the apostle Paul, perhaps we can find again our real identity as the people of God. Indeed, we do discover our identity when we find what we cannot keep off our minds.

Paul and Timothy (1:1).

The salutations in the letters of the apostle Paul are always fascinating. They often reveal remarkable insights for the community of faith.

From our viewpoint, Timothy's name should probably not appear in the first verse. Perhaps a word from him near the end would seem appropriate, but not at the outset as one of the principal authors.

Obviously Paul wrote this letter. He may have dictated it to his younger colleague. This esteemed senior minister had no cause to give such prominent attention to his assistant. Yet, here in the opening words, Timothy is recognized as an equal with Paul. In this relationship, there is a deep sense of the corporate nature of the church. Paul is not alone in his imprisonment at Rome. His faithful companion is by his side. The worth of this younger minister is affirmed, and his importance in the mission of the church is underlined when the aging apostle begins the letter, "Paul and Timothy."

Servants of Christ Jesus (1:1).

Paul establishes the nature of his ministry and the direction of the mission of the church with his chosen title—*servant*. In other letters Paul finds it necessary to defend his position as an apostle, but not so with the Philippians. They do not question the apostolic authority of their beloved pastor.

But why does Paul maintain he is a servant—really a slave? (*Slave* is the meaning of *doulos,* the word used in the original text.) Paul sees himself as more than a servant who is free to come and go. He identifies himself as a *slave*, one in the possession of his master forever. He is subject to Christ's will and owes Christ complete obedience.

The servant role also identifies Paul with his Lord, who "took upon him the form of a servant" (2:7 KJV). The servant role of Christ is the role Paul sees for himself, and for the church.

This is hard for us to comprehend. Not many of us are taking our continuing education in experiences that will enable us to be servants. But this was our Lord's choice—and Paul's.

In his Gospel, John senses beautifully this thrust of Christ's ministry. He points out that when Jesus was most aware of his power, the cosmic sweep of his ministry, "knowing that the Father had given all things into his hands, and that he had come from God and was going to God" (John 13:3), he took not a sword nor a sceptre, but a towel and basin and washed his disciples' feet.

This image seems forever to be in Paul's mind—the servant role.

We need to recall frequently, in the midst of our schedules and programs, that the church is only true to its heritage—it is only relevant—when it assumes the role of the servant. Servanthood makes Paul's ministry authentic, and so it is with us.

Saints (1:1).

This word is even more perplexing than servant. Who is saintly? Who wants to be! For most of us, a saint is one encased in the beautiful, stained-glass windows of some great cathedral. Yet, this is a word of great importance for us. We must discover what it means. In the New Testament, saints are those set apart from others in the sense that they are dedicated to a new way of life. They are not saints because of their own virtue; they are saints because God has called them and set them apart to serve. They are "saints in Christ Jesus."

We are saints when our relationship to Jesus Christ sets us apart. Why are we different? Because we are in Christ. My concordance reveals that in Paul's letters the words "in Christ Jesus" are used forty-eight times, the phrase "in Christ" thirty-four times, and "in the Lord" fifty times.

We are not "set apart" to put us out of touch with our world or with folks around us. We are set apart as a special people, "a chosen race," to be the servants of God after the manner and mind of our Lord.

Grace and peace (1:2).

The Philippian letter begins and ends with *grace*. Dr. Thomas Langford points out that the letter is basically about grace, with the word at the beginning and the end, as if all the rest of the letter is a parenthesis expanding on the concept. William Barclay makes the interesting observation that Paul has taken the normal greeting phrases of two great nations and molded them into one.[2] "Grace" *(charis)* is the usual Greek salutation, while "peace" *(eirēnē)* is a frequent Hebrew greeting. But Paul has taken the two and added his own dimension in the light of the Christian faith.

"Grace" *(charis)* basically means joy and beauty, associated with the idea of charm, but here Paul speaks of the love of God manifested in the coming of Jesus. There is a beauty in life which comes from a new relationship with God through Christ—the relationship of grace.

"Peace" *(eirēnē)* is the fruit of this new relationship. Reconciliation with God brings a sense of health and wholeness. It is far more than the absence of trouble. Through Christ, God makes whole what has been divided. Broken relationships are healed. Those who experience the grace of God know of forgiveness which brings unity.

When Paul greets his friends with the words *grace* and *peace*, he is praying that they shall know the joy of being reconciled to God through Christ, and that, as a result, the peace of God might bring new relationships to God and with all God's family.

These opening words begin to help us find our identity with Christ. We are to follow in the way of our Lord who saw himself supremely as a servant. We are called by Christ to be saints, a part of the family of God set apart to serve. We are recipients of grace as we experience God's forgiveness and mercy, which, in turn, brings wholeness and unity to our broken lives and relationships. There is a sense in which this greeting is the theme of the letter. But there are yet further dimensions to probe.

Partnership in the gospel (1.5).

The Philippians help Paul comprehend the meaning of partnership. In the beginning of his ministry Paul is something of a loner. He is looked upon with suspicion because he persecuted

[2]William Barclay, *The Letters to the Philippians, Colossians, and Thessalonians,* (Philadelphia: Westminster, 1959), p. 15.

Christians. Soon, Paul finds that the nature of the faith is really community. It is interesting to note that he never uses the singular for the word *saint*—always *saints*. We are in fellowship, in partnership, in community.

No wonder Paul gives thanks for these folks. They minister to him and his needs. Though he is with them but a short time in the initial life of the congregation, they follow him across the years and help him in so many ways.

It is clear that a special relationship exists between Paul and the Philippians. He says to them, "You are always in my heart" (1:7, TEV). They are his "beloved" (2:12); his "joy and crown" (4:1). Sharing takes on new meaning for Paul, and he sees how pivotal such a relationship is for a church.

This is the idea we have in mind today when we say the style of leadership in the church must be participatory. As Paul puts it in the Roman letter, "mutually encouraged by each other's faith, both yours and mine" (Romans 1:12). Paul finds added strength in his ministry when it is shared with great laymen, like Barnabas, with younger ministers like Mark and Timothy, with lay women like Lydia, and with ordained women like Phoebe (Romans 16:1). He discovers he needs people with whom he does not always agree, such as Simon Peter. Out of all of this diversity there develops a kind of partnership which gives strength and an enriched dimension to that early church.

These early Christians, though often very different in background and point of view, are drawn together because of the gift of grace and the work they are called to do together. Their partnership transcends barriers because they are one in Christ. This kind of partnership (*koinonia*) creates a strong church and is critically needed for us to bear a meaningful witness today.

He who began a good work in you will bring it to completion (1:6).

Nothing is more characteristic of our Lord's call to discipleship than an admonition to grow. In the beginning, God's redeeming grace brought this church into being. Paul never claims to be founder of this church. God originated the church, and God's grace will continue until the ultimate completion. The stress is on God's continuing faithfulness. God who began a good work will not allow the church to wind up on the scrap heap. And God continues to perform the work of redemption. In spite of all suffering and internal conflict, the community will be preserved, and so the readers are called to be faithful and stand firm (1:27).

Love . . . with knowledge (1:9).

After giving thanks for the sense of community that has grown out of a common goal, Paul prays for love to grow in that fellowship. The love for which he prays is not mere sentimentality, but love which grows in knowledge and perception. The idea is that love with perception is needed "to have a sense of what is vital" (1:9, Moffatt). In a community where there has been some disunity and fault-finding (see Philippians 4:2,3), a spirit of love, based on a better knowledge of God and God's ways, will bring greater understanding and harmony in the congregation.

A paramount need in all of our churches is "love . . . with knowledge" (1:9). The Body of Christ must experience love which is disciplined by knowledge and discernment. Here we see the critical role of a nurturing ministry in the church.

In a visit to our church in Norway, I saw this emphasis in a new way. Methodism is a minority church in Norway The state church far exceeds United Methodist membership. I discovered that our small United Methodist churches had a much larger percentage of members in attendance at worship services. In fact, while the state church has about 2 percent of membership in worship services, United Methodist congregations frequently exceed 50 percent of the membership in attendance. The influence of our congregations is far beyond their numerical strength. The sense of loyalty is very evident. Commitment to significant social ministries is amazing for churches of such small membership. For a time I struggled to understand the reason.

I discovered that training for confirmation in the church covered a period of at least a year and frequently a longer period of intensive study. Emphasis is placed on biblical studies and theological understanding. To be a part of a minority church calls for careful and thorough grounding in the faith. No wonder attendance is held at a high percentage. There is reason for a high level of commitment to ministries of love and justice. These folks are experiencing "love with knowledge." They have a reason for the faith that is in them, and that faith works in services of love.

Our local churches must give high priority to our nurturing role. In a time like ours we must have Christians who have experienced "love with knowledge."

At this point let's pause and examine the letter thus far (1:1-11). A review of the total message brings a startling conclusion. This is not only a letter to a first-century Christian community; it is our letter. It addresses the situation we confront every day in the mission of the church.

We have been reminded that we are recipients of the gift of God's grace. That is what initiates a church. We are a redeemed and redeeming community. We are not alone in our ministry in the congregation. Christ is at work in our church. This is not just a human institution. We are in partnership with Christ, and with those Christians who are in the pilgrimage with us. Our Lord seeks to impact us with his mind and spirit, and calls us to manifest the love which we have come to know in him—a love that enables us to discover what really matters in our mission.

This letter is no ancient period piece! It forces us to look at the life of our church in the light of the mind of Christ. We must submit our programs, budgets, and long-term goals to the exposure of the mind that was in Christ.

As we read these words we take new hope for our church. The Spirit is at work with us to lead us from narrow, provincial, and perhaps misdirected concerns. In a world so at odds with the mind of Christ, we are called to demonstrate the truth of this transforming gospel. We who have received the gifts of grace and peace are now summoned to respond to these gifts of love in concrete thoughts and actions. Our agenda is the mind of Christ in the church today. That kind of agenda may bring new life to all we do as we seek to discover how we, as individuals, can bear our witness, and how our congregations can really be a part of accomplishing God's mission today.

For Discussion at the Close of Chapter 2

1. What must we do as modern disciples to express our calling to servanthood?

2. Who are some of the servants of Christ that you know in the church today?

3. As the Body of Christ today, how do we deal with a secular society? Do we have a sense of being "set apart"?

4. What evidences do you see of an understanding of partnership in our church?

5. What experiences have made you feel that you are growing in your spiritual life and developing in discipleship?

3

Proclaiming the Gospel of Christ

Philippians 1:12-26

Following the introductory greetings, Paul moves into the major thrust of his letter. He wants his friends to know about his situation. He is in prison, probably in Rome, nearing the end of a demanding career, apparently facing death. One would expect a sad story from a doomed man. Certainly the Philippians are anxious, not only about Paul's welfare but about the whole future of the Christian mission. The imprisonment and possible death of the major leader of the faith could well mean a fatal blow to this young movement.

The tone of Paul's approach to this crisis is nothing less than amazing. He faces reality. He is not looking for escape or an easier life. He understands that the Christian faith does not always lead to personal comfort. His own fate is not his major concern. He is primarily interested in the future of the Christian mission. He affirms a faith that has sustained him personally and that can undergird the Christian cause as it faces trial and adversity. Let us look more carefully at this courageous affirmation of faith.

What has happened to me has really served to advance the gospel (1:12).

Paul faces what certainly appears to be the end of his work, but a surprising God uses an apparent calamity to open a whole new phase of the Christian mission. Perhaps no one is more surprised than Paul!

From Paul's experience in prison, new dynamics come to work in the proclamation of the faith. His contacts with the "praetorian guard" open a new channel of communication. The famous Imperial Body Guards, some 10,000 stationed in Rome, are exposed to this unusual man, and they catch something of the contagion of his faith. Evidently some of the guards tell the story of this faith which dominates their strange prisoner. The old, old story, which Paul's words tell so well, along with his courageous actions, continue to be related in a whole new segment of Roman society. What surprising things happen when faithful people tell the story that has meant so much to them!

But another dimension of ministry develops. "Most of the brethren have been made confident in the Lord . . . and are much more bold to speak the word of God without fear" (1:14). The example of Paul stimulates others to proclaim the word. In the Phillips paraphrase, he describes these folks as "taking fresh heart in the Lord from the very fact that I am a prisoner for Christ's sake" (1:14, Phillips).

This is a dramatic development in the saga of that first-century community. The proclamation of the faith is not just the privilege of a select few. The priesthood of all believers is emerging.

The courage of Paul overflows and empowers otherwise reticent people to speak the word of God without fear. We must always be alert to the impact of our lives upon those about us. We make a tremendous difference as we give evidence of the power of the gospel. One man, facing the tragic end of his own work, lived so gallantly that the Christian church entered a new chapter in history—the apostolate of the laity.

But another strange element becomes a part of the proclamation issuing from Paul's captivity. Some "proclaim Christ for their own ends, with mixed motives, intending to annoy me"

(1:17, Moffatt). It is difficult to comprehend what Paul is experiencing. There may have been, among those preachers, some who proclaimed Christ but called upon converts to maintain Jewish laws and customs. Paul confronted this problem previously and had dealt with it rather sharply in the Galatian letter, but now he faces the issue differently. He helps us in dealing with the wide diversity we often see in the church today.

What really matters, says Paul, in the final analysis, is that "Christ is proclaimed" (1:18). He does not care for the interpretation of the gospel preached by some of these folks. He even raises a question about their motives. But his overarching concern is being fulfilled. All that matters is that Christ is preached.

Here is a word so sorely needed in our church today when clergy and laity become polarized over differences of opinion. We almost form armed camps and take up battle with one another in the community of faith. Paul gives us some handles for this problem. He rises above personal resentment and jealousy. He is unwilling to do battle just because some preachers are enhancing their own prestige. He is not particularly upset when some of these folks are unfriendly to him. Some try to steal the show while he is in an obscure spot—a prison! But, what matters? Only one thing—"Christ is proclaimed; and in that I rejoice!" (1:18).

The gospel must always be proclaimed by imperfect people. Yet, facing even that unpleasant fact, we can look at the whole matter with some insight and understanding which is a part of love (1:9). Many folks will do many good things, though they may not do them our way. This offers a word of counsel to preachers and congregations. Look at the overall impact of life and ministry. Don't get caught up in a quarrel over every minor detail. Choirs will never be angelic. Some ushers may be crude. Administrative boards will often be obstinate. Congregations will not and should not follow every beck and call of the minister. Preachers will have their bad days and go off on tangents. We are all fallible. We can all look for imperfections, and at times we all make a lot over some very little things.

What is the big thing in the church? What really matters? The joy that Christ is proclaimed and that we can all bring our differences together and be a part of Christ's mission. If we can rise above the tyranny of things that do not matter and center on the essentials, we can be the people of God in work and witness. What is the big thing? The proclamation of the good news of the grace of God made known in Jesus! Even in the midst of differences, the power of the Spirit can work in the church and use human beings to do what matters most—proclaim the gospel in word and in concrete deed and action.

To me to live is Christ (1:21).

Here is the secret of Paul's ability to experience stress, imprisonment, conflict, and even face his possible execution with clear eyes and a calm spirit of faith. He has found a reason for living which permeates his entire being. Today's English Version translates the word this way: "For what is life? To me, it is Christ" (1:21, TEV).

Paul's relationship with God in Christ gives him a sense of freedom even behind bars. It enables him to confront his dilemma with confidence and strength. He believes that whatever happens to him will be for the best. If he is sentenced to death and faces the executioner, he will be ushered into the presence of Christ. If he lives on to face difficult situations, then he will continue to witness and work for Christ. His desire is not to live on for his own sake, but for the purpose of forwarding the Christian mission. "It is much more important," he declares, "that I remain alive. . . . I will stay on with you all, to add to your progress and joy in the faith (1:24-25, TEV).

Paul is sustained in this time of anxiety by two things—the prayers of his friends at Philippi, and the "help which comes from the Spirit of Jesus Christ" (1:19, TEV).

Again, what a partnership! Paul is strengthened by prayers

from the community of faith and by power from the presence of Christ. Many of us can witness to the fact that repeatedly we have been affirmed and upheld in such a fellowship with God and God's people. It is an almost unbelievable experience, but across the years the people of God have drawn upon strength from each other and from the continuing assurance that God never leaves us alone. Life is no longer a lonely way; it is fellowship with God.

A reason for living! How critical it is for all of us. Paul's reason is Christ. He is literally immersed in the mind and spirit of Christ. As a bird lives in the air, as a fish lives in water, so Paul is in Christ and never feels separated from his presence.

This is the gospel of Christ we are called to proclaim. We can witness to the sustaining grace which we have discovered in Christ.

> Fear not, I am with thee;
> O be not dismayed,
> For I am thy God,
> And will still give thee aid;
> I'll strengthen thee, help thee,
> And cause thee to stand,
> Upheld by my righteous,
> Omnipotent hand.[3]

---

[3]"K" in Rippon's Selection, 1787.

For Discussion at the Close of Chapter 3

1. Do you feel that the church today gives proper attention to the priesthood of all believers or "the apostolate of the laity"?

2. What reasons do you see for the polarization in the Christian community today—liberals versus conservatives, social action oriented versus evangelicals, etc.?

3. How do we decide what positions in the Christian church are open to compromise and which ones must be affirmed as basic and kept at all cost?

4. What sustains you in times of stress and anxiety?

5. What do you see as the major task for the church today?

4

What Christ Expects of His Church

Philippians 1:27–2:18

This portion of the letter must be seen as a unity in which the people who have experienced God's grace are summoned to live up to their high calling. The theme for the passage is well stated: "The important thing is that your way of life should be as the gospel of Christ requires" (1:27, TEV). We shall look at what Paul understands to be the responsibility of persons who seek to have "the mind of Christ." What does Christ expect of the church?

Stand firm in one spirit with one mind (1:27).

The Philippian church is set in the midst of an alien world. The standards of this tiny group of Christians are constantly challenged. This new faith is too demanding in its requirements not to confront opposition and even hostility.

Paul calls the church to stand firm with a sense of unity. Often evil is strong and the odds seem overwhelming. In such times Christians must present a strong united front. Let the opposition see the strength of Christian forces who stand together supported by superhuman resources.

Never is it suggested in the New Testament that the Christian life or the role of the church is an easy one. From the very first day it has been tough for the Christian community in Philippi. Paul understands that. He, too, is having it hard. We are "engaged in the same conflict" he says (1:30). It is an honor to suffer for Christ, he maintains. As Christians, we cannot countenance cruelty, injustice, greed, and threats to freedom. We must stand together, firm for our faith. We must suffer, if need be, as we work in the Christian community. We are Christians under the cross, sharing our Lord's struggle if we belong to Christ.

The truth was so vividly brought to mind in our 1982 visit for the Seventy-fifth Anniversary of Methodism in Estonia in the Soviet Union. Our largest United Methodist local church in Europe is located in Tallinn, the capital of Estonia. In spite of hardships and limitations, United Methodist churches are crowded. On two successive evenings, meeting in a Lutheran building, which is the Kaarli Church, United Methodist congregations numbered 1,800 and 2,000. In the mother church, the Merepuistee Church, which seats only 450, the actual attendance count at 9 AM on Sunday was over 800 with aisles and vestibules jammed for a 3½-hour service of celebration and ordination.

In the midst of all of their problems, the choral and congregational singing was fantastic. The emotional impact of sharing in such a service was overwhelming. At the close of one of those stirring anniversary services, David Bridge, the representative of British Methodism, said to me, with tears streaming down his cheeks, "I say, old boy, that was a bit much."

There are still places where the Christian witness is tested, and where the role of the church is not an easy one. We must always remember wherever we are in mission that we are Christians under the cross.

Unity and Humility (2:1-4).

The greatest danger which constantly confronts the church is not opposition from without. It is always dissention and disunity from within. What the forces of Satan cannot accomplish in persecution, they bring to pass by disrupting concord and harmony within the fellowship.

Divisiveness in the church must be dealt with, or the healthiest church will falter in mission. The apostle suggests several practical ways of working through such conflict.

His first suggestion is that the members of the congregation forget themselves. "Do nothing from selfishness or conceit" (2:3). There are always folks, even in the church, who seek prestige. They sometimes first experience the faith with such enthusiasm that they become very assertive. All of us can be victims of spiritual pride.

The antidote for this problem is clear. "Count others better than yourselves" (2:3). This is never easy to do. True recipients of God's grace and forgiveness should give evidence to the kind of humility that enables one to look beyond the shortcomings of others.

Humility is such a fragile attribute that to claim it almost means that we do not possess it. It is like the man given a pin by his Sunday school in recognition of his humility, and who later had it taken away from him because he insisted on wearing it.

Humility becomes increasingly essential as one grows in the Christian life and as leadership opportunities are given in the life of the church. My pastor of Kentucky high school days, Dr. Frank C. King, never allowed me to forget that in my ministry. Following my election to the episcopacy he took me aside and said, "Ed, I've noticed that when some people are elected to the episcopacy, they grow. Others just swell. Those of us who love you have the highest hopes that you will grow." Then, in his inimitable way, he cackled, poked me at the waistline, and said, "You've swelled enough." I was keenly aware that he referred not to my growing waistline, but to the size of my hatband! I hope I will never forget that vivid exhortation!

This passage helps us to remember that the one who deserved highest exaltation chose servanthood and the humble way of life.

Paul calls his friends to have the same mind (2:2). He is referring to harmony of life and spirit, not a uniformity of thinking. Paul recognizes the richness of diversity in the church.

We do not want the deadness of conformity in our fellowship. This is always a threat to life and vitality in the church. We do need to bring our differences together and negotiate until we discover that upon which we can agree. Then with a sense of unity and with the same great goals, we can proceed to act. This kind of unity in diversity brings credit to the church, and praise to a God who made us all different, but a part of one great family of love.

The other solution prescribed by Paul is, "Let each of you look not only to his own interests, but also to the interests of others" (2:4). We have a tendency to be intent on our own affairs, our own rights, and our own achievements. In the Christian church we must be concerned about the good of the whole fellowship. Here, again, is the partnership theme, living with each other in the spirit of love which we have seen in the attitude of Jesus Christ.

The Supreme Example (2:5-11).

No nobler picture of Jesus is found anywhere in the Bible than in this passage, known as "The Christ Psalm." It probably was a part of an early Christian hymn or an affirmation of faith. The fullness and richness of the life and ministry of Jesus is richly portrayed.

For me, this is the key passage in the entire letter. The rest seems to expand on the meaning of this marvelous mind and spirit of Christ. The central core of the gospel is contained in this passage. It recounts Christ's coming to earth, his life and sacrificial death, and his Lordship for the church and for all creation.

If there is any incentive for unity and humility in the church, it is found in this picture of our Lord. Paul points out that Jesus was in the "form of God," that he possessed both the image and glory of God. Even though he enjoyed equality with God, he declined to grasp it and, rather, embraced the will of God which meant servanthood, humility, suffering, and a cross.

Many Bible scholars believe Paul is making a parallel between the first Adam and the second Adam. The first Adam sought to exploit his situation and tried to grasp equality with God. The second Adam, Christ, renounced his right, though he could have seized it. He chose, instead, suffering and a cross. The result of his choice is that "God has highly exalted him and bestowed on him the name which is above every name, that at the name of Jesus every knee should bow, in heaven and on earth and under the earth, and every tongue confess that Jesus Christ is Lord, to the glory of God the Father" (2:9-11).

The message is that one who refused to grasp his own right, and become obedient to death and suffering, is now highly exalted. The dignity that was his right he did not clutc, and he is now elevated to his rightful place because of his submission to sacrifice. He is acclaimed above all and now receives worship and honor as the Lord of all of life.

Now, says Paul, look at that mind and attitude that was in Christ and have it in yourself and in your relationships with your fellow beings. All this complex theology is set forth to say, "Now, Christians, go and do the same!" The humility and servanthood seen in Christ if evidenced in your life will enable you to triumph over the petty divisions which threaten the wholeness of the church.

As a general superintendent in the church who hears so often the plea for "promotion," and "upward mobility," and who himself often enjoys the privilege of high office, this passage becomes a strong word. God exalts the downward reach of servanthood and not the upward grasping so often evident in much of our ministry today. This word is for us. It is our letter! It is food for our lives that is not easy to digest. God still exalts those who choose to serve!

There is another important word in this passage. Paul is deeply grateful for the love and affection extended toward him by the Philippians. It is cause for real joy. But, Paul's joy will not be complete (2:2) until he knows that the mind and spirit of

Jesus has so permeated this congregation that divisiveness has vanished and there is unity and wholeness in the fellowship. When this word is received, Paul's cup of joy will be filled to the brim and will overflow.

This is what Christ expects of the church. Christ wants us to be so receptive to divine grace and so permeated by the Spirit, that his purposes and plans will be made known by and in us. It is a high goal, but Christ calls us to no less.

Therefore, my beloved, as you have always obeyed . . . work out your own salvation (2:12).

The whole point of the Christ Psalm was our Lord's obedience to the purpose of God (2:8; see also Hebrews 5:8). The example of the obedient Christ is now applied to the Philippian church. Christ obeyed and so should you! It is almost an order with military overtones, except that it is softened by the address "my beloved." Paul exhorts the church to obey in his absence as they did when he was present with them. How easy it is to live on a high level when one is in our midst who inspires such response. Paul hopes that this letter will stir up memories of better days that will revive such behavior.

Obedience is called for a purpose, that of completing God's work in them. "Work out your own salvation," Paul says. Has Paul changed his theological position of salvation by faith alone? Not at all. Here, as always, one must look at the entire word.

God has begun a good work in this congregation. God's presence and grace continues. The completion of the work of God in the church cannot be accomplished by humanity alone. But, we must not resist God's work in our lives and in our fellowship. We depend upon God's grace for growth. God is busy at work with us and in us, but we must cooperate with God in producing the fruits of the Christian life. Do this, obediently, says Paul, and there will be no more evidence of divisiveness in the congregation.

Christ's desire for our church is that there be within it both the action of God and the response of God's people. It is again the emphasis on partnership—God plus us, or, as Paul put it previously, "For to me to live is Christ." The two are inseperable if we are to have a relevant, meaningful church.

Without grumbling (2:14).

Here immediately following a passage that exalts the suffering servant, Christ, who won the exaltation of God and is proclaimed Lord of all, you come upon this word *grumbling*. Rather incongruous, it seems! It is an interesting word in the Greek—*goggusmos*. It means the muttering of a mob about to be in rebellion. What can it mean here? It is likely that it refers to folks who never rise above negativism. They want to debate and dispute everything. Nothing is ever right. Everything is flawed.

Grumbling in the church did not cease in the first century! We still have it with us. The grumbler sours the sweet milk of Christian fellowship. But, even worse, the grumbler destroys his or her own spiritual life. Thanksgiving is forgotten. All life is poisoned with self-interest. Again, we must look to the mind and attitude of Christ for the answer. Only the mind of Christ can free the grumbler from the shackles of captivity to a negative approach to life.

Among whom you shine as lights in the world (2:15).

Here is what Christ expects of the church! Rising above the self-centeredness of grumbling, the Christian possessed of the mind of Christ becomes a shining light "in the midst of a crooked and perverse generation" (2:15).

Just as the church at Philippi is set in the midst of a hostile world, so we must bear our witness in a morally corrupt society.

We are called as the people of God to reflect the one who is the Light of the world. The darkness of a distorted sense of values casting gloom over all our world calls for a church responsive to the words of our Lord, "You are the light of the world" (Matthew 5:14).

A church which is a light-bearer, which holds "fast the word of life" (2:16), will not only bring joy to Paul's heart (2:17–18), but it will begin to make a difference in the surrounding world. It has happened in Philippi. It is happening in Rome due to the example of Paul and his associates, and it can happen in our time. A church true to its mission can impact the trends of the time, the decision-making process in our communities, and the entire moral climate of our day. The very existence of a church conforming to the mind and attitude of Christ is a light in darkness. We can be such a church if we reflect the love of God in the demonstration of our own lives.

Not many people ever heard of The United Methodist Church in Kristiansund, Norway. During our visit there in September 1982, the young pastor, the Reverend Oyvidn Helliesen, told us a dramatic story from the history of that small but growing church. Earlier in this century, a Russian fishing vessel weathered a severe storm on the North Sea. The ship made port at Kristiansund since several crew members had been injured during the ordeal.

One of the crew, a boy in his late teens, Faan Puskay, had broken his leg and had other severe injuries. The ship could not wait for him to recover and left Faan in the hospital in a strange land with customs he did not understand and a language he did not speak. It must have been a lonely, painful experience for a young boy.

A faithful Methodist pastor began to visit Faan regularly, and when he was able to leave the hospital, the pastor found a place for the boy to stay with a Methodist family. Faan's interest in the church grew. He was converted to the Christian faith and felt called to preach the gospel.

The Methodist pastor and congregation at Kristiansund encouraged this direction for Faan's life. They raised money to send him to school in Great Britain. After his training, Faan returned to visit his benefactors and told them of reports of a young growing Methodist Conference in his homeland of Estonia. Again the church encouraged him and helped Faan with his fare to return to his home for his ministry.

Faan Puskay became a devoted Estonian Methodist minister, giving leadership to his church through the terrible years of war, persecution, and suffering. On the wall of the Kristiansund Church there is a plaque telling the story of Faan Puskay.

I preached at Kristiansund on September 29, 1982, and told them of my plans to go on to Estonia. The faces of the older members were radiant. They stood and waved to me, telling me to take warm greetings to Faan.

On Saturday, October 16, 1982, I led a Bible study from Philippians for a crowded room of preachers in Tallinn in Estonia. I told the story of Faan Puskay and brought greetings from his friends at Kristiansund. In the back of the room an old man, quite wrinkled and worn, now in his eighties, stood and walked toward me with tears streaming down his cheeks. Of course, it was Faan Puskay. He hugged me as I think I've never been hugged before. You can imagine the emotion of that moment and the rejoicing of that group of preachers.

Here was a pastor and a church of very small membership which had become "a light-bearer" for a lonely, young boy. The light had continued to shine until that boy became a stalwart leader in the Christian struggle in one of the real frontiers of the Christian faith. So we are called to "shine as lights in the world." This is the only way the darkness will be overcome.

Timothy (2:19), Epaphroditus (2:25).

Here again emerges the vitality of "partnership in the gospel." Just as soon as some word of his own future is received,

Paul intends to send Timothy to Philippi and if possible come himself. In the midst of Paul's trying, lonely experience of incarceration, Timothy shares the apostolic concerns. He is a faithful and trusted companion.

Here we confront Paul's only complaint in his letter. He refers to other associates and says, "They all look after their own interests, not those of Jesus Christ" (2:21). This may well mean that some of Paul's followers are primarily concerned about their own business and welfare. As the length of Paul's confinement grows, these former co-workers find more important things to do than support him. The greatest of God's servants faces depression as conditons change, and as solitude increases. But— Timothy stands by! His supportive role in this relationship makes him not only a valued companion but a trusted messenger.

The name of Epaphroditus also adds great meaning to this fellowship. He had been the bearer of the gift to Paul from the Philippian church. During his visit in Rome he had been seriously ill. Now that he is on the way to recovery he longs to be home again. Paul sends him back with regret but with deep appreciation. He says, "He nearly died for the work of Christ, risking his life to complete your service to me" (2:30). The verse literally means, "He gambled with his life." Here is the story of another humble person, little known to us, who proved his fidelity in the midst of hardship. Church history is full of such folks who are "known only to God."

There is quite a contrast between Timothy and Epaphroditus. One obviously talented, able, intelligent, a part of the "first team," the other, a humble servant. Both served the cause with distinction and commitment. Both had a significant part in bolstering Paul's courage in a time of trial. Both were an important part of the partnership of that early church. These are the kind of folks, diverse though they may be, who bring richness and meaning to the church. The various parts make up the whole and bring unity to the church.

How grateful many of us are for people who bring hope and encouragement at a critical point in our lives. Obviously Epaphroditus came with the gift of love from the Philippians at a crucial time in Paul's prison experience.

We all give thanks for such folks who came bearing gifts of love, time, and companionship. I recall the latter days of my high school experience in Kentucky. I did so want to go to college to pursue studies for the Christian ministry. It seemed an impossible dream. It was 1934-35 in the midst of the depression. We all did well to keep alive, let alone find funds for education. Very few of my classmates even thought about college.

In the midst of discouragement and almost despair, a great Methodist layman came my way. His name was Mayo M. Taylor, a decendant of the distinguished missionary, Dr. Charles Taylor, who had gone to China from the Methodist Episcopal Church, South, in 1848. The grandson, Mayo, was a layman and not at all a man of means. He never allowed me to get my eyes off college. He helped me get a scholarship to Kentucky Wesleyan College. He brought me great books to enlarge my mind and stretch my vision. He took me to great meetings, one where I heard for the first time Bishop Arthur J. Moore and Bishop A. Frank Smith. Mayo saw me off on the day I left for college. The first letter I received during those homesick days was from him.

Across the years this beloved, brilliant man kept in touch with me and delighted in the progress I made. I discovered that he did the same for others. His enthusiastic faith always kept his local church in touch with places where ministry was needed.

For the most part Mayo Taylor will be a name "known only to God," but for some of us, he was like Epaphroditus, giving unselfishly of himself to be caring and supportive.

In summary, what does this portion of the letter say about our mission today? It sets out some of the fundamental attitudes required of those of us who belong to the community of faith. Christians must have a manner of life as the gospel requires (1:27). Christians must present a united front. We are living in a time when our fragmented witness weakens the entire cause of Christ. While we stand firm, we do not do so with any sense of arrogance. We are called to live above selfishness and conceit. Real Christian humility evidenced in the life of the congregation establishes unity of life and spirit.

Proclamation is always at the heart of the ministry of the church, but it must be more than a vocal exercise. It must be a message expressed in concrete deeds and action. Words alone will never have an impact on a society bent on making money, seeking prestige, and enjoying affluence. Such a time calls for evangelists who take the message of the gospel beyond the walls of the sanctuary. The need is for caring persons who express Christ's outlook of servanthood in a secular-oriented, uncaring society. The word we declare must literally be a "word of life."

Possessing these qualities akin to the mind of Christ will not only give us a sense of unity within the church, but it will enable us to "shine as lights in the world" (2:15). The Christ, whose suffering servanthood is so graphically portrayed in this passage, calls for the same mind and attitude in the Christian community today.

The success of the church is not judged finally by the size of our budgets and buildings, but by the way in which our encounter with Christ has fundamentally changed our outlook on life, and our commitment to serve a hurting world.

For Discussion at the Close of Chapter 4

1. What evidences do you see of unity in the Body of Christ today?

2. How can we "stand firm" in our faith without compromise and yet keep unity in our local church?

3. What steps do we need to take to strengthen the evangelistic outreach of our church?

4. Recall some humble person who influenced your life for good. Think of ways we might do the same for persons in some critical situation today.

5. What does your church do to express a caring ministry in your own community?

5

What It Means to Know Christ

Philippians 3:1-21

The theme for this section of the letter is set out in Paul's declaration: "All I want is to know Christ" (3:10, TEV). For Paul, this was without question the major goal of his life and the all-consuming purpose for the Christian community. But what does it mean to know Christ? This passage certainly gives some clear directions.

Rejoice in the Lord (3:1).

The constant emphasis on joy in this letter from prison is nothing less than amazing. Paul is threatened with longer confinement or death. The Philippians faced severe trials. Yet, here is this emphasis on joy—a kind of indestructible joy. The basis for it makes the difference. It is not a joy coming from fortunate or comfortable circumstances. It is not a response to some bit of good news. It is, in fact, a joy coming in the midst of grim circumstances.

Paul is dealing here with *joy in the Lord.* The presence of Christ in his life and in the community of the faithful makes the difference. Much that comforts and consoles has been taken away. Threats and terrors abound. Yet the presence of Christ was enough to cause Paul to rejoice and to call again and again for his friends to share in the joy of the Lord. This is what it means to know Christ. There is in the life of a Christian a joy that cannot be taken away.

Dr. Barclay illustrates this truth with a story from early Methodist experiences.

> John Nelson was one of Wesley's most famous early preachers. He and Wesley carried out a mission in Cornwall, near Land's End, and Nelson tells about it. "All that time, Mr. Wesley and I lay on the floor: he had my greatcoat for a pillow, and I had Burkitt's notes on the New Testament for mine. After being here near three weeks, one morning about three o'clock Mr. Wesley turned over, and, finding me awake, clapped me on the side, saying: 'Brother Nelson, let us be of good cheer: I have one whole side yet, for the skin is off but one side!' " They had little enough even to eat. One morning Wesley had preached with great effect: "As we returned, Mr. Wesley stopped his horse to pick the blackberries, saying: 'Brother Nelson, we ought to be thankful that there are plenty blackberries; for this is the best country I ever saw for getting a stomach, but the worst I ever saw for getting food!' "[4]

Neither Wesley nor Paul were deterred by the discomforts of life. To know Christ brings joy—not the hilarious, laughter kind of joy but the contentment which comes from knowing Christ and being united with him (4:11–12).

Paul is not afraid of repetition in his letters. He had written previously to the Philippians about joy, and he does it again in this letter. The experience of the "joy in the Lord" saves him again and again, and he wants this fundamental truth to be emphasized in the church. Is this not a major teaching of our Lord, who prays that his joy might remain in us that our joy might be full (John 15:11).

---

[4]William Barclay, *The Letters to the Philippians, Colossians and Thessalonians,* (Westminster Press: Philadelphia, 1959), pp. 64-65.

Whatever gain I had, I counted as loss for Christ (3:7).

Knowing God through Christ goes far beyond observing the rites and rituals of the church. In fact some of Paul's contemporaries were still trying to bind Christians with the obligations of the Old Covenant. Paul has some very strong words for these folks (3:2).

Paul keeps the Law. He has a rich heritage in the Jewish tradition (3:2-6). He discovers in his encounter with Christ, and in his succeeding pilgrimage, that salvation comes not from keeping all of the Law and ritual—salvation comes by grace alone. Paul can never explain how Christ entered his life, but he knows it happened on the Damascus Road, and that nothing else matters now. Christ found him. And all of the rest—his human attainments and his self-righteousness—are cast aside as "mere garbage" (3:8 TEV). He has no righteousness but that which comes from God, and his whole aim and direction in life is changed.

That I may know him (3:10).

Paul's every power is directed toward knowing Christ "and the power of his resurrection" (3:10). The verb used in this text for *to know* indicates a personal knowledge. It is more than an intellectual grasp. It is not the knowledge of any set of creeds or principles. Paul's aim is not to know certain facts about Christ, but to know Christ as a person, in a relationship of personal faith and fellowship.

To know Christ in this personal experience is the greatest gain Paul can imagine. The results of such personal knowledge are well expressed in the old gospel hymn by W. T. Sleeper:

> Out of my bondage, sorrow and night,
> Jesus, I come, Jesus, I come;
> Into Thy freedom, gladness and light,
> Jesus, I come to Thee.

Out of my sickness into Thy health,
Out of my want and into Thy wealth,
Out of my sin and into Thy self,
Jesus, I come to Thee.

Forgetting what lies behind, and straining forward to what lies ahead (3:13).

Knowing Christ keeps us from getting "stuck fast in yesterday." Memories are often a source of blessing, but we can easily stunt our spiritual growth by dwelling on past sorrows, mistakes, and even victories. While appreciating all that is positive about the past, the prize in Christian living is not even in present achievements but in "the upward call of God" (3:14). Knowing God calls for the incessant "straining forward."

Earlier in this book I mentioned my visit to our church in Estonia in the Soviet Union for the celebration of their Seventy-fifth Anniversary. There I met the saint and patriarch of Estonian Methodism, Aleksander Kuum, who was for many years Superintendent of Methodist work there. At the height of the purges under Stalin, Kuum, who was a respected leader of wide influence, was arrested and sentenced to Siberia. There he stayed for more than five years, only to be released following the death of Stalin.

Now retired, but still the predominant figure there in Methodism, Kuum spoke at the Seventy-fifth Anniversary Jubilee at Tallinn. His message was magnificent. There was little dwelling on past sufferings and hardships. The dominant note was one of joy and the awesome challenge for the future for the church in Estonia.

In a quiet, personal moment I spoke, through an interpreter, with Aleksander Kuum. I asked him about the sufferings of the Siberian imprisonment. He smiled warmly and replied, "I lost my arthritis in Siberia. The dry climate cured it and now in my eighties I'm not troubled with it at all." I suggested that I was not really ready to try the Siberian climate to cure the arthritis in my knee. He laughed heartily and responded,

"Well, you will just have to continue to be unhealthy!"

Kuum's dynamic, radiant spirit has held Methodism together in trying times. With him there is no dwelling on the past. He calls his church to "press on toward the goal for the prize of the upward call of God in Christ Jesus" (3:14).

I press on toward the goal for the prize of the upward call of God in Christ Jesus (3:14).

Knowing Christ is not just an initial experience. Conversion does not immediately bring one a new environment or a developed inner life. Growth in Christ is essential. To come to know Christ calls forth an experience of continuing knowledge. We are called to grow in grace and in the knowledge of our Lord Jesus Christ.

Paul's personal union with Christ began with his conversion on the Damascus Road. Then followed thirty-three years of growth in Christ. He continued to grow with an intense desire. He was a focused man with one priority. In his letter to the Philippians, he calls his friends to the same pilgrimage with the same high objectives. With vigorous, athletic figures of speech he calls for Christians "with hands outstretched" (3:13, Phillips) to strain forward toward the prize of the upward call of God in Christ. Our destination as Christians is not some particular place, but a new way of looking at life—the "Christ way."

The Christian life is not an easy one. It calls for strength in heart, mind, and soul. Growth toward maturity must never end. As Paul admonishes, "Let those of us who are mature be thus minded" (3:15).

Paul Tournier, the physician possessed of such spiritual insight, once said, "I have retired. . . . But the spiritual life does not require retirement! I am still listening in to God, to what he has to say to me today, and tomorrow, and the day after all the tomorrows, until the final and total revelation of the resurrection."

Growth requires a desire on our part. It involves intentional steps. It is never final; it never ends. The local church can provide opportunities for continuing growth in discipleship. In the Body of Christ we can learn to grow together. God is at the center of our support community. As we grow in grace and grow together spiritually, we can be a part of accomplishing God's mission today. There are tremendous tasks to perform, and only mature Christians sharing in partnership with Christ can bear effective witness today.

> Be strong. We are not here to play,
> to dream, to drift:
> We have hard work to do
> and loads to lift;
> Shun not the struggle—
> face it,
> 'Tis God's gift. Be strong!
> —Maltbie D. Babcock

Our commonwealth is in heaven (3:20).
We are citizens of Heaven (3:20, Phillips).

Here lies the Christian's highest loyalty. Philippi was a Roman colony. It was a strategic military center, lying as it did between Asia and Europe. The Roman military dominated this community. Roman laws were observed and Roman customs followed.

Paul is saying that just as Roman colonists never forget where their citizenship actually is, so Christians must never forget that they are citizens of the kingdom of heaven. There lies our supreme loyalty. Our conduct must forever reflect the one we serve and the one to whom we really belong.

Paul closes this section on what it means to know Christ by sounding the note of Christian hope (3:21). He declares that the day will come for the one who knows Christ when frail humanity

will be changed into nothing less than the divinity of Christ—
"his glorious body." Those who know Christ realize that life
does not end up on the scrap heap, but rather in the presence of
the splendor of God's eternity.

What does it mean to know Christ? It means that by the gift of
grace, life has been set in a new direction. Old aims and goals are
forgotten. Life takes on new meaning. Our utmost desire is to
move with vigor and determination toward the goals of Christian
living and to become more and more alive to the presence of
Christ within us and within God's world.

The process of knowing God always begins with an encounter
with God through Christ. Then, the redeeming power of God
continues with us to enable us to "press on" toward maturity.
Seeking the mind and attitude of Christ, we move, although
sometimes with hesitations and setbacks, toward the goal—
maturity with Christ.

The pilgrimage to know God through Christ is always accom-
panied by hope. Trials, persecutions, and misunderstandings
may be a part of the way but the conclusion is not in doubt. The
God who proved that Calvary can issue forth in Easter morning
is in this pilgrimage with us. We are part of a resurrection
society, and the God who empowered the new life at Easter will
bring to pass eternal purposes for us. Because Christ lives, we
shall live also! (John 14:19).

For Discussion at the Close of Chapter 5

1. What specific expression do you see of "the joy of the Lord" in your church?

2. What do you consider to be the priorities of your local church?

3. What new ways of looking at life have you discovered as a result of your Christian pilgrimage?

4. What is the source of highest loyalty for the Christian community?

5. How do you see our present-day church as a "part of a resurrection society"?

6

Christ and the Future

Philippians 4:1-23

As this letter nears its close, the future is much on the mind of Paul and also of his readers. His own future is in question. At the very best this venerable soldier of the cross does not have many years. The future of the church is a matter of concern. Persecution is ever present. Disunity threatens the Body of Christ. The final admonitions of the letter deal very much with how the Christian community faces what lies ahead.

Stand firm in the Lord (4:1).

While some commentators believe this verse to be the conclusion of the message of the previous chapter, it seems to me to be most appropriately associated with Paul's closing exhortations. His beloved followers, whom he calls "my joy and crown," are called to "stand firm." The Greek word translated "crown," *stephanos,* was the designation for the wreath awarded the victor in an athletic contest. Paul wants his friends, in that final day, to know the triumph and joy of victory in the Christian race. When he completes his own earthly pilgrimage, Paul desires this beloved congregation to be a part of his victor's wreath, his reward at the end of the way.

Perhaps no admonition is more appropriate for the church today. Attacks upon the validity of the church are frequent.

Serious questions are raised about the whole future of the Christian movement. Questions about the direction of the mission of the church come from many sources. Perhaps there have been few times in history when the future of the Christian church all over the world seems more threatened. We hear the continuous bad news of membership decline. While good news comes from some parts of the world about church growth, the word in the mainline churches of the western world is not very encouraging.

Paul reminds us that there is a victory to be won. We are in a tough race that calls for endurance. The church is called to remain faithful and obedient to the Lord to the end. Our faith rests in Christ alone, and it is our confidence that we can do all things in Christ who strengthens us (4:13). We are called to a steadfast allegiance to Christ. Here is a call for us to do more than "go to church." It is a summons to "be the church." Faithfulness to Christ can still bring the church to a day of victory when "every knee should bow . . . and every tongue confess that Jesus Christ is Lord" (2:10-11). The crown of triumph awaits Christians who remain faithful.

Whose names are in the book of life (4:3).

The future does not belong to the famous, the strong, the affluent, or the glamorous. These qualities may get our name in *Who's Who* or the social register. It remains for the faithful to have their names written in the "book of life." Those listed in this book have received the gift of God's grace and have given themselves in the servant role to God and God's people.

What surprises there may be when one day the book is opened! We may understand what our Lord meant when he said the last shall be first and the first, last. Those often regarded as great will be stricken with surprise when God's list places first the poor widow who gave all she had when the offering plate was passed. The future belongs to the faithful!

Rejoice in the Lord always; again I will say, Rejoice (4:4).

We have already noted that joy is one of the predominant themes of this letter. There must be no misunderstanding, "Rejoice . . . *and* again I say, Rejoice" (KJV). Paul, who is caught up with the Philippians in "the same conflict" (1:30), calls for joy in the midst of opposition and suffering. Joy is the hallmark of any real church.

Anne Herbert of Spartanburg, South Carolina, spent eighteen years of her life as a devoted servant of Methodism, teaching nurses in China. She was forced to leave in 1943 as the Revolution spread. In 1982, she returned to what is now The People's Republic of China to visit friends and former associates. They went early one Sunday to Moore Memorial Church in Shanghai. Long before the service began the church was filled with people. They were singing as the congregation gathered. The first song she heard from this congregation whose church had been closed for thirty years was, "I Need Thee Every Hour," and then they burst into singing "Rejoice, Ye Pure in Heart." A bit later the hymn was "Joyful, Joyful, We Adore Thee."

No one will ever know what these Christians endured following the closing of the Christian church all over China. During the so-called Cultural Revolution, Bibles and hymnals had been destroyed. But, some kept the faith! Today the church is alive and growing, singing hymns of joy. Their song is not one of regret or bitterness. It is, "Rejoice, give thanks, and sing!"

So the church is marked by joy.

Have no anxiety about anything, but in everything by prayer and supplication with thanksgiving let your requests be made known to God (4:6).

Christian joy finds its basis in prayer and thanksgiving. The possibility and reality of prayer and thanksgiving keeps us from being destroyed by fears and anxieties. It enables us to realize that "the Lord is at hand" (4:5).

Here must be a major concern for every church. We must cultivate in our churches a concern for and practice of prayer which exalts thanksgiving and puts fears and worries in their proper place. I think Georgia Harkness did not overstate the case in the opening sentence of one of her finest books: "Of all the things the world now desperately needs, none is more needed than an upsurge of vital, God-centered, intelligently grounded prayer."[5]

The needs of the world are many and varied. In the church we can survive without many things we sometimes think essential, but we cannot live and bear effective witness without prayer. It has often been said that prayer is the greatest force in the universe and the one least utilized. For joyful witness and meaningful mission we must be people of prayer. This is our hope for the present and the future.

The peace of God . . . will keep your hearts and your minds in Christ Jesus (4:7).

Isn't it strange that Paul uses a military term to talk about peace? The words "will keep" are best translated "shall keep guard over." The Philippians knew about Roman soldiers maintaining a guard or protection over their city. God's peace, says Paul, will protect "your hearts and minds."

Jesus found his peace in union with God. God's peace was his gift to the church. This peace guards the minds and hearts of members of the church and enables us to keep the unity of the faith and be witnesses to God's order in our lives.

Let us recall that Paul is speaking to the corporate life of the church. A relationship of peace with God will enable the church to be a reconciling force in the world. God's peace in our hearts gives to the church joy and strength for witness in a warring world.

[5]Georgia Harkness *Prayer and the Common Life* (Nashville: Abingdon-Cokesbury Press, 1948), p. 13.

Think about these things (4:8).

In the opening chapter of this book I quoted from Archie Ammon's poem which declared:

> . . . You have your identity when you find out not what you can keep your mind on but what you can't keep your mind off.

Paul has learned in prison that you keep your life in proper direction by your thoughts. He could have groveled in bitterness and despair. That is the way to lose direction. He is speaking from a lesson well learned when he says, "Whatever is true . . . honorable . . . just . . . pure . . . lovely . . . gracious . . . if there is any excellence, if there is anything worthy of praise, think about these things" (4:8).

The thoughts and meditations of our inner lives determine our direction, our destiny. "Your life is shaped by your thoughts" (Proverbs 4:23, TEV).

So much that is cheap, tawdry, ugly, and degrading fills the minds of many of us today. Glued to the sordid and superficial, we miss so much of the beauty and holiness of life. Paul calls the church to live with the great positive themes of the Christian life and spirit. In his translation, Goodspeed says, "Let your minds dwell" on these high levels. In other words, Christians do not just visit the high ground occasionally. They dwell there.

Our future literally depends on what we keep on our minds today.

I rejoice (4:10).
I have learned, in whatever state I am, to be content (4:11).
I can do all things in him who strengthens me (4:13).

The casual observer might not expect such words from a prisoner in Rome. They explain the source of real contentment which possesses Paul as he faces a precarious future.

Paul expresses his gratitude for the gift the Philippians sent to him by Epaphroditus. He is counting his blessings. He is grateful not only for the gift and the service of the messenger, but he is deeply gratified by the generosity in the hearts of the people. He is touched by their care and concern. Opportunities to assist him are not always available, Paul says, but he is overjoyed that this congregation shares again in his tribulations. Above all, Paul is grateful to God who inspires and motivates the beneficence of the church.

While he is deeply gratified over the Philippians' gift, Paul reminds his friends that outward conditions do not set the agenda for his life. Facing hunger or abundance, want or plenty, Paul possesses an inner calm that saves his sanity. "I have learned, in whatever state I am, to be content" (4:11).

Paul's contentment arises not from a passive or fatalistic attitude toward life. He is never contented with things as they are (3:14). He is contented because he takes every day, receiving what comes, from God's hand. He is not shackled by outward events, good or bad. He has at the center of life the gift of God's grace which gives him a unique freedom. Christ lives in him, so he can announce to all: "I can do all things in him who strengthens me" (4:13). Paul never claims to be self-sufficient. He is adequate for what comes because Christ is a reality in his life.

As God supplies his needs, God provides for his people in their need. "My God will supply every need of yours according to his riches in glory in Christ Jesus" (4:19). But, the church must always remember that God uses human instruments to supply needs. The Philippians are used of God to care for Paul's situation. Other human hands had also undergirded the great apostle.

We must not see this word as an invitation to relax our own efforts. If the grace of God is in us, we will be pleasing to God as we use our opportunities and abilities to share with others "a fragrant offering, a sacrifice acceptable and pleasing to God" (4:18). If the Spirit of God, which enables us to bear fruit, is in our lives, then we will share the gifts of love. The fruits of our Christian living give authenticity to the presence of God in our lives. The church that claims the presence of the Spirit in her midst will evidence that reality in meeting needs far beyond the confines of the local congregation.

All the saints greet you (4:22).

As this letter closes we see again an expression of the corporate life of the church. One sister church sends greetings to another. Already in the first century, there is a sense of connection among Christian churches. They share concerns, exchange visitors, pray for each other, and are beginning to realize some sense of unity in the entire Body of Christ.

We also see that this letter is meant for the entire church, not just a few leaders. The church at Philippi receives a word of good news as reference is made to greetings from members of the Roman Church who are in some way related to Caesar's household. This probably does not refer to the personal family of Caesar, but to the guards in the Imperial Service who had some contact with Paul through his own guards in the prison. It is a source of great encouragement for Paul to report that the gospel is winning its way into the heart of the Roman government.

When one church is struggling and facing persecution, it is great news to hear that the faith is penetrating the administration of the empire. For these early Christians facing a questionable future, this word of triumph gives them new heart. The gospel is, indeed, on the way to influencing people all over the world.

The grace of the Lord Jesus Christ be with your spirit (4:23).

The letter ends as it began, with *grace*. The prayer of Paul for his "joy and crown," his "dearly beloved" saints at Philippi is that the grace, which had brought him safe thus far, might sustain these dear friends in their pilgrimage until the ultimate victory.

For Discussion at the Close of Chapter 6

1. What is your basic conviction about the future of the Church as we know it today?

2. Do you feel that the church in the United States is sufficiently vital to survive persecution similar to that experienced in many countries of the world?

3. What do you do to make prayer a vital force in your life and the mission of your church?

4. Is the kind of peace mentioned in Paul's letter (Philippians 4:7) possible today?

5. How can this "peace of God" relate to peace in our world?

6. What suggestions can you make to shape your church more from the mind of Christ?

Conclusion

Paul has conveyed to his friends at Philippi something of what it means to have the mind of Christ in the life of the church. The overall impact of the letter illustrates that the people of God, everywhere in all circumstances, should celebrate their faith with joy. The joy that Jesus found in union with God, the joy Paul knew from being "in Christ," is the hope for the church.

The English clergyman L. P. Jacks once wrote, "Christianity is the most encouraging, the most joyous, the least repressive of all the religions of mankind. While it has its sorrows and stern disciplines, the end of it is a resurrection, not a burial—a festival and not a funeral."[6]

Celebration from a prison may seem ridiculous, but the triumphant faith of the apostle is not restricted by bonds. This is the faith that is the gift of God's grace, and the faith that has been victorious for Christians across the centuries. Such faith calls for unbroken fellowship with Christ.

When we embrace Christian discipleship we find that we are caught up in a fellowship which enables us to face any contingency. A faith-union with Christ ushers us into a partnership with God and with Christians near and far. We, too, are then able

---

[6]J. Wallace Hamilton, *Horns and Halos in Human Nature* (Tappan, N. J.: Revell, 1954), p. 54.

to proclaim, "I can do all things in [Christ] who strengthens me" (4:13).

> Lord, give me such a
>   faith as this;
> And then, what e'er may
>   come,
> I'll taste, e'en now the
>   hallowed bliss,
> Of an eternal home.
>   —William H. Bathurst

References for Additional Study

Barclay, William. *The Letters to the Philippians, Colossians, and Thessalonians. The Daily Study Bible.* Philadelphia: Westminster, 1959.

Carter, Thomas. *Life and Letters of Paul.* Nashville: Cokesbury, 1921.

Dietrich, Suzanne de. *Toward Fullness of Life; Studies in the letter of Paul to the Philippians.* Philadelphia: Westminster, 1966.

Ensley, Francis Gerald. *Paul's Letters to Local Churches.* New York: Women's Division of Christian Service, Board of Missions of the Methodist Church, 1956.

Harrell, Costen J. *The Radiant Heart: Studies in Paul's Letter to the Philippians.* New York: Abingdon-Cokesbury, 1936.

Hunter, Archibald Macbride. *The Letter of Paul to the Galatians; the Letter of Paul to the Ephesians; the Letter of Paul to the Philippians; the Letter of Paul to the Colossians.* Vol. 22, *The Layman's Bible Commentary.* Richmond, Va.: John Knox, 1959.

Harmon, Nolan B., ed. "The Epistle to the Philippians." In vol. 11, *The Interpreter's Bible.* Nashville: Abingdon, 1955.

Keck, Leander E. "The Letter of Paul to the Philippians." In *Acts & Paul's Letters.* Vol. 7, *Interpreter's Concise Commentary.* Nashville: Abingdon, 1983.

Martin, Ralph P. *The Epistle of Paul to the Philippians; an Introduction and Commentary.* Vol. 11, *Tyndale New Testament Commentaries.* Grand Rapids, Mich.: Eerdmans, 1960.

Rainy, Robert. *The Epistle to the Philippians*. Vol. 21, *The Expositor's Bible*. New York: A. C. Armstrong, 1903.

Vincent, Marvin R. *A Critical and Exegetical Commentary on the Epistles of the Philippians and to Philemon*. New York: Scribners, 1897.

Weaver, Horace R., ed. "Philippians." In *The International Lesson Annual, 1979-1980*. Nashville: Abingdon, 1979.

Wesley, John. "Forty-Four Sermons." Chapter 35, "Christian Perfection." London: Epworth, 1977.

THE LETTER OF PAUL
TO THE
PHILIPPIANS

1 Paul and Timothy, servants [a] of Christ Jesus,

To all the saints in Christ Jesus who are at Philippi, with the bishops [b] and deacons:

2 Grace to you and peace from God our Father and the Lord Jesus Christ.

3 I thank my God in all my remembrance of you, 4 always in every prayer of mine for you all making my prayer with joy, 5 thankful for your partnership in the gospel from the first day until now. 6 And I am sure that he who began a good work in you will bring it to completion at the day of Jesus Christ. 7 It is right for me to feel thus about you all, because I hold you in my heart, for you are all partakers with me of grace, both in my imprisonment and in the defense and confirmation of the gospel. 8 For God is my witness, how I yearn for you all with the affection of Christ Jesus. 9 And it is my prayer that your love may abound more and more, with knowledge and all discernment, 10 so that you may approve what is excellent, and may be pure and blameless for the day of Christ, 11 filled with the fruits of righteousness which come through Jesus Christ, to the glory and praise of God.

12 I want you to know, brethren, that what has happened to me has really served to advance the gospel,

[a] Or *slaves*   [b] Or *overseers*

1. 1: Acts 16. 1, 12–40; Rom. 1. 1; 2 Cor. 1. 1; Gal. 1. 10; Col. 1. 1; 1 Thess. 1. 1; 2 Thess. 1. 1; Philem. 1.
1. 2: Rom. 1. 7.   1. 6, 10: 1 Cor. 1. 8.
1. 7: Acts 21. 33; 2 Cor. 7. 3; Eph. 6. 20.   1. 12: Lk. 21. 13.

13 so that it has become known throughout the whole praetorian guard[c] and to all the rest that my imprisonment is for Christ; 14 and most of the brethren have been made confident in the Lord because of my imprisonment, and are much more bold to speak the word of God without fear.

15 Some indeed preach Christ from envy and rivalry, but others from good will. 16 The latter do it out of love, knowing that I am put here for the defense of the gospel; 17 the former proclaim Christ out of partisanship, not sincerely but thinking to afflict me in my imprisonment. 18 What then? Only that in every way, whether in pretense or in truth, Christ is proclaimed; and in that I rejoice.

19 Yes, and I shall rejoice. For I know that through your prayers and the help of the Spirit of Jesus Christ this will turn out for my deliverance, 20 as it is my eager expectation and hope that I shall not be at all ashamed, but that with full courage now as always Christ will be honored in my body, whether by life or by death. 21 For to me to live is Christ, and to die is gain. 22 If it is to be life in the flesh, that means fruitful labor for me. Yet which I shall choose I cannot tell. 23 I am hard pressed between the two. My desire is to depart and be with Christ, for that is far better. 24 But to remain in the flesh is more necessary on your account. 25 Con-

---

c Greek *in the whole praetorium*
1. 13: Acts 28. 30; 2 Tim. 2. 9.
1. 19: Acts 16. 7; 2 Cor. 1. 11.   1. 20: Rom. 14. 8.
1. 21: Gal. 2. 20.

vinced of this, I know that I shall remain and continue with you all, for your progress and joy in the faith, 26 so that in me you may have ample cause to glory in Christ Jesus, because of my coming to you again.

27 Only let your manner of life be worthy of the gospel of Christ, so that whether I come and see you or am absent, I may hear of you that you stand firm in one spirit, with one mind striving side by side for the faith of the gospel, 28 and not frightened in anything by your opponents. This is a clear omen to them of their destruction, but of your salvation, and that from God. 29 For it has been granted to you that for the sake of Christ you should not only believe in him but also suffer for his sake, 30 engaged in the same conflict which you saw and now hear to be mine.

2 So if there is any encouragement in Christ, any incentive of love, any participation in the Spirit, any affection and sympathy, 2 complete my joy by being of the same mind, having the same love, being in full accord and of one mind. 3 Do nothing from selfishness or conceit, but in humility count others better than yourselves. 4 Let each of you look not only to his own interests, but also to the interests of others. 5 Have this mind among yourselves, which you have in Christ Jesus, 6 who, though he was in the form of God, did not count equality with God a thing to be grasped,

4 Or *slave*
1. 28: 2 Thess. 1. 5.   1. 30: Acts 16. 19–40; 1 Thess. 2. 2.
2. 1: 2 Cor. 13. 14.   2. 3–4: Rom. 12. 10; 15. 1–2.
2. 5–8: Mt. 11. 29; 20. 28; Jn. 1. 1; 2 Cor. 8. 9; Heb. 5. 8.

7 but emptied himself, taking the form of a servant,[d] being born in the likeness of men. 8 And being found in human form he humbled himself and became obedient unto death, even death on a cross. 9 Therefore God has highly exalted him and bestowed on him the name which is above every name, 10 that at the name of Jesus every knee should bow, in heaven and on earth and under the earth, 11 and every tongue confess that Jesus Christ is Lord, to the glory of God the Father.

12 Therefore, my beloved, as you have always obeyed, so now, not only as in my presence but much more in my absence , work out your own salvation with fear and trembling; 13 for God is at work in you, both to will and to work for his good pleasure.

14 Do all things without grumbling or questioning, 15 that you may be blameless and innocent, children of God without blemish in the midst of a crooked and perverse generation, among whom you shine as lights in the world, 16 holding fast the word of life, so that in the day of Christ I may be proud that I did not run in vain or labor in vain. 17 Even if I am to be poured as a libation upon the sacrificial offering of your faith, I am glad and rejoice with you all. 18 Likewise you also should be glad and rejoice with me.

19 I hope in the Lord Jesus to send Timothy to you soon, so that I may be cheered by news of you.

2. 9–11: Rom. 10. 9; 14. 9; Eph. 1. 20–21.

2. 13: 1 Cor. 15. 10.   2. 15: Mt. 5. 45, 48.

20 I have no one like him, who will be genuinely anxious for your welfare. 21 They all look after their own interests, not those of Jesus Christ. 22 But Timothy's worth you know, how as a son with a father he has served with me in the gospel. 23 I hope therefore to send him just as soon as I see how it will go with me; 24 and I trust in the Lord that shortly I myself shall come also.

25 I have thought it necessary to send to you Epaphroditus my brother and fellow worker and fellow soldier, and your messenger and minister to my need, 26 for he has been longing for you all, and has been distressed because you heard that he was ill. 27 Indeed he was ill, near to death. But God had mercy on him, and not only on him but on me also, lest I should have sorrow upon sorrow. 28 I am the more eager to send him, therefore, that you may rejoice at seeing him again, and that I may be less anxious. 29 So receive him in the Lord with all joy; and honor such men, 30 for he nearly died for the work of Christ, risking his life to complete your service to me.

3 Finally, my brethren, rejoice in the Lord. To write the same things to you is not irksome to me, and is safe for you.

2 Look out for the dogs, look out for the evil-workers, look out for those who mutilate the flesh. 3 For we are the true circumcision, who worship God in spirit,* and glory in

* Other ancient authorities read *worship by the Spirit of God*
3. 3: Rom. 2. 28–29; Gal. 6. 14–15.

Christ Jesus, and put no confidence in the flesh. 4 Though I myself have reason for confidence in the flesh also. If any other man thinks he has reason for confidence in the flesh, I have more: 5 circumcised on the eighth day, of the people of Israel, of the tribe of Benjamin, a Hebrew born of Hebrews; as to the law a Pharisee, 6 as to zeal a persecutor of the church, as to righteousness under the law blameless. 7 But whatever gain I had, I counted as loss for the sake of Christ. 8 Indeed I count everything as loss because of the surpassing worth of knowing Christ Jesus my Lord. For his sake I have suffered the loss of all things, and count them as refuse, in order that I may gain Christ 9 and be found in him, not having a righteousness of my own, based on law, but that which is through faith in Christ, the righteousness from God that depends on faith; 10 that I may know him and the power of his resurrection, and may share his sufferings, becoming like him in his death, 11 that if possible I may attain the resurrection from the dead.

12 Not that I have already obtained this or am already perfect; but I press on to make it my own, because Christ Jesus has made me his own. 13 Brethren, I do not consider that I have made it my own; but one thing I do, forgetting what lies behind and straining forward to what lies ahead, 14 I press on toward the goal for the prize of the upward call of God in Christ Jesus.

3. 4–7: Acts 8. 3; 22. 3–21; 23. 6; 26. 4–23; Rom. 11. 1; 2 Cor 11. 18–31.

15 Let those of us who are mature be thus minded; and if in anything you are otherwise minded, God will reveal that also to you. 16 Only let us hold true to what we have attained.

17 Brethren, join in imitating me, and mark those who so live as you have an example in us. 18 For many, of whom I have often told you and now tell you even with tears, live as enemies of the cross of Christ. 19 Their end is destruction, their god is the belly, and they glory in their shame, with minds set on earthly things. 20 But our commonwealth is in heaven, and from it we await a Savior, the Lord Jesus Christ, 21 who will change our lowly body to be like his glorious body, by the power which enables him even to subject all things to himself.

4 Therefore, my brethren, whom I love and long for, my joy and crown, stand firm thus in the Lord, my beloved.

2 I entreat Euodia and I entreat Syntyche to agree in the Lord. 3 And I ask you also, true yokefellow, help these women, for they have labored side by side with me in the gospel together with Clement and the rest of my fellow workers, whose names are in the book of life.

4 Rejoice in the Lord always; again I will say, Rejoice. 5 Let all men know your forbearance. The Lord is at hand. 6 Have no anxiety about anything, but in everything by prayer and supplication with

3. 17: 1 Cor. 4. 15–17.   3. 21: 1 Cor. 15. 35–58; Col. 3. 4.
4. 3: Lk. 10. 20.

4. 6: Mt. 6. 25–34.

thanksgiving let your requests be made known to God. 7 And the peace of God, which passes all understanding, will keep your hearts and your minds in Christ Jesus.

8 Finally, brethren, whatever is true, whatever is honorable, whatever is just, whatever is pure, whatever is lovely, whatever is gracious, if there is any excellence, if there is anything worthy of praise, think about these things. 9 What you have learned and received and heard and seen in me, do; and the God of peace will be with you.

10 I rejoice in the Lord greatly that now at length you have revived your concern for me; you were indeed concerned for me, but you had no opportunity. 11 Not that I complain of want; for I have learned, in whatever state I am, to be content.

12 I know how to be abased, and I know how to abound; in any and all circumstances I have learned the secret of facing plenty and hunger, abundance and want. 13 I can do all things in him who strengthens me.

14 Yet it was kind of you to share my trouble. 15 And you Philippians yourselves know that in the beginning of the gospel, when I left Macedonia, no church entered into partnership with me in giving and receiving except you only;

16 for even in Thessalonica you sent

4. 9: Rom. 15. 33.
4. 10: 2 Cor. 11. 9.   4. 13: 2 Cor. 12. 9.
4. 16: Acts 17. 1–9; 1 Thess. 2. 9.

me help *f* once and again. 17 Not that I seek the gift; but I seek the fruit which increases to your credit. 18 I have received full payment, and more; I am filled, having received from Epaphroditus the gifts you sent, a fragrant offering, a sacrifice acceptable and pleasing to God. 19 And my God will supply every need of yours according to his riches in glory in Christ Jesus. 20 To our God and Father be glory for ever and ever. Amen.

21 Greet every saint in Christ Jesus. The brethren who are with me greet you. 22 All the saints greet you, especially those of Caesar's household.

23 The grace of the Lord Jesus Christ be with your spirit.

---

f Other ancient authorities read *money for my needs*
4. 23: Gal. 6. 18; Philem. 25.

About the Author

Edward L. Tullis received the A.B. degree from Kentucky Wesleyan College and the B.D. (M. Div.) degree from Louisville Presbyterian Theological Seminary. He also was awarded the Doctorate in Humane Letters from Kentucky Wesleyan College and the Doctorate in Humanities from Claflin College. The degree of Doctor of Divinity was awarded by Union College and Wofford College. His wife is the former Mary Jane Talley, whom he married on September 25, 1937, and they have a son and daughter.

Now a bishop in The United Methodist Church, Edward Tullis has served local churches in the cities of Louisville, Lawrenceburg, Irvine, Frankfort, and Ashland, in Kentucky. He once served as Associate Secretary, Section on Church Extension, Division of National Mission of the Board of Missions. Before serving as Resident Bishop, Nashville, Area, Bishop Tullis served as Resident Bishop, Columbia Area, The United Methodist Church.

Bishop Tullis has written various magazine and newspaper articles. *Shaping the Church from the Mind of Christ* is his first book. It has grown out of his deep desire to write a devotional study for ministers and lay groups that would provide exposure to the content in Philippians as it relates to current directions for the ministry and mission of the church.

About the Painting on the Cover

The painting on the cover of this book is titled *Survived the Storm*. The creation of this art was a very painful experience for me.

I painted this piece during a time when I felt rejected—very hurt by my peers. I realized I was feeling anger both at them and at myself because we seemed unable to communicate. I finally started to paint, and the actual painting process became an act of prayer. I cried. I poured all my feelings out to God as I painted. I named myself before God.

As I painted, a storm emerged within me with all its fury. I was in the middle of the storm—battered and broken by the angry sea. But God did not leave me there! As I named myself before God, God began to name me in the midst of my storm. I felt God's presence real within me. I felt the assurance of God's love for me. I felt the courage to speak out—not to be afraid—to depend on God for strength. At that time, I began to paint light breaking into my storm—surrounding me, holding me up, loving me, not letting me go under.

When I finished the painting, I had a deep peace, a confidence that no matter what storms might rage in my life, God would always be there holding me up.

JERRY DUNNAM